The Journal of a Six-Time Stroke Survivor

DARRELL L. CRAFT

ISBN 979-8-88644-585-5 (Paperback)
ISBN 979-8-88644-586-2 (Digital)

Covenant Books
11661 Hwy 707
Murrells Inlet, SC 29576
www.covenantbooks.com

To my wife, Carol Craft.

Thank you for standing by my side through all of it.

PROLOGUE

My name is Darrell Lee Craft, and my big break in social work came in August 2002. I was hired as the psychological services coordinator in the Allen County (Ohio) Jail. I had been working in human services-related jobs for almost ten years and had served in the US Navy in intelligence for just over six years.

Despite my nerves during the interview because there were so many people present, Daniel W. Beck, the individual serving as Allen County sheriff at the time, had hired me. At thirty-eight years old, I finally would be making enough money to live like I wanted to live. I could even afford to raise a family, if I should choose to start one.

It would be September 2011 before I would get married to Helen Carol Gallaspie. She had been widowed and had three children. They were Seth Allen Gallaspie, Selah Rose Gallaspie, and Melody Sol Gallaspie. We initially rented a house for about six years, but we eventually bought our own home. We moved in on the day after Christmas in 2017.

*****

I have a master's degree in social work from the Ohio State University and independent licensure as a social worker and an endorsement in clinical supervision of social workers from the state of Ohio. As part of the sheriff's office, I used to be certified in correctional healthcare by the National Commission on Correctional Healthcare, and additionally in the past, I held four certifications from the International Critical Incident Stress Foundation including *Emergency Services, Spiritual Care in Crisis Intervention, Mass Disaster and Terrorism,* and *Schools and Children Crisis Response.* I also was an approved instructor in *Group Crisis Intervention* and in *Individual Crisis Intervention and Peer Support* with the International Critical Incident Stress Foundation. I was also a member of the West Central Ohio Critical Incident Stress Management Team led by Rick Skilliter, who was the chief of police for the Bluffton, Ohio, Police Department. Furthermore, I also advised the 46.1 Response Ohio Team in the Assemblies of God Church. The leader was Terry Hunt, an Assemblies of God pastor as well as a personal friend.

My career was going well and reached its peak in 2018. On my fifty-fourth birthday in January 2018, I was quoted in an article on page one of the *Lima News* in Lima, Ohio, about drug and alcohol treatment. My photograph was also published. About five months later, I finished writing a book titled *The Sheriffs of Allen County, Ohio: 1831 through 2017*. The Allen County Sheriff's Office had it published and only fifty copies were printed, but it was still my first book. Later that year, I was named Civilian Employee of the Year for 2018 for the Allen County Sheriff's Office.

It seemed like I was on top of the world in 2018, but my career would end up having a horrible cost for me. The additional stress from this seeming success contributed to an already too stressful job being even more stressful. This likely contributed to my six strokes.

The following pages are the story of my six strokes, and how God carried me through them. After God put it in my heart to write this story after my fourth stroke, I started by writing about events that I knew I would want to remember in the form of short essays. St. Rita's Medical Center, in Lima, Ohio, has a brain injury support group. I wrote a six-page presentation about my experiences, and it was read at a support group meeting by Megan Evers, SLP, a speech therapist, whose verbal presentation skills are so much better than mine after the strokes. The presentation went well, and a lot of good discussions ensued. When the presentation was over, I rewrote it. I remembered a little bit more and added this information too. I rewrote this presentation eight times in total. Each time, I remembered a little more. Then God moved me to complete the grueling task of reviewing over one thousand pages of medical records, even with two distinct cases of double vision. The updated presentation seemed to follow the flow of the medical records, but there were parts of which I still had no memory. On those parts, I summarized medical records and filled in the blanks. The following manuscript of my experience with having six strokes emerged.

CHAPTER 1

On the night of December 21, 2018, while I slept, I had my first of six strokes. My first stroke was originally misdiagnosed as depression by the hospital because I had a bizarre and extremely realistic dream about shooting myself in the head at about 3:00 a.m. one night, shortly before I went to the hospital for the first time. Additionally, the hospital staff misdiagnosed my condition because of a lack of information. They did not complete a comparison CT scan with contrast of my head and neck because I had an allergic reaction to the barium dye that was used to detect a kidney stone that I had about thirty years earlier while I was in the US Navy. Since they did not complete this test, they did not have the information that would have detected my first stroke.

The so-called depression that I was experiencing was actually a brain stem stroke. It was either a small cerebellar ischemic stroke or a pontine ischemic stroke. My first stroke was one of these two types, and the second stroke that I would have later during the next month was the other type.

There is really no way to determine which stroke occurred first.

Statistics from the National Center for Biotechnology Information claim that thirty percent of survivors of brain stem strokes die within a year. The National Center for Biotechnology Information also reports that one-third of survivors become dependent on others for their daily living activities.

When I became sick, my wife encouraged me to write my symptoms down in case she had to take me to the hospital while I was unconscious. These written notes of my symptoms have become a valuable record to me. Besides my dream of shooting myself in the head, I was extremely forgetful. I could not remember how to get to my family Christmas party. I had to try to drive the route in advance. Eventually, I had to return home while I could still remember how to get home. I then had to carefully map out the location of the party in advance of it.

I also could not remember if my wife's family Christmas party had been in the morning or the evening on Christmas Day. During this time, I remember asking myself if I had a stroke. I remember thinking that I did not have a stroke because I would have been in more pain and I would have had more memory loss. I also experienced headaches and some blurriness in my vision. It felt like my right eye was turning clockwise in my head. I remember this happening a couple more times, but it was not as bad as the first time it happened.

My vision was extremely blurry unless I closed my right eye. The paperwork after my second stroke said that I was negative for double vision at that time. The double vision would play prominently into the symptoms of my strokes in the future, but it apparently was not a factor yet. I also had some numbness in my lips, face, and teeth.

I hallucinated a lot and felt like I saw the people attending Christmas Eve service at church either appearing or disappearing. I also saw what I thought was tobacco juice running down from the ceiling. I also saw black, fuzzy spots on the ceiling. On one occasion, I remember seeing a shadow on the ceiling. I remember that my hallucinations stopped before New Year's Day.

*****

I finally went to urgent care on New Year's Day. A nurse from the sheriff's office, Michelle Magness, LPN, was concerned about me and called the jail doctor, Dr. John Biery at home and asked him to order tests. He did this since it was New Year's holiday; and Dr. James Bowlus, my regular family doctor, was not available. Dr. Biery sent me to urgent care, and the urgent care staff sent me to the emergency room of St. Rita's Medical Center.

*****

The staff of St. Rita's Medical Center thought I was depressed because of my dream of shooting myself in the head. Since they did not complete the comparison CT scan with contrast, they misdiagnosed my condition. I finally convinced the hospital staff that I was not suicidal, so they released me. They referred me to a psychologist, but the appointment was eventually canceled because I was in the hospital following my second stroke.

*****

When I was released from the hospital, I felt like I was detached from the world, both physically and emotionally. I remember going to the retirement reception of Michael Schoenhofer, the man who was retiring as the director of the Mental Health and Recovery Services Board of Allen, Auglaize, and Hardin counties several days after my trip to the hospital. I remember standing in line to wish him well, but I felt trapped in confusion, and no one seemed to understand.

*****

These symptoms occurred about the time that I switched from a CPAP machine to a BiPAP machine to deal with my sleep apnea, so I initially thought that the change of machines could have been the cause of my problems. I remember that Jennifer Jacobs, PA-C, who was monitoring my pulmonology, ordered an echocardiogram to make sure my BiPAP machine was working well for me. No problems were found, but I continued to feel confused.

*****

The emergency department had me see Dr. Bowlus. Dr. Bowlus was a Christian and was extremely supportive and involved in my case in the coming years, but at that time, he accepted the reports from my emergency room experience as factual. He seemed focused on determining whether I was depressed. I did not know how to communicate how I felt. This was frustrating to me.

*****

I remember my neck hurting extremely badly. I went to my chiropractor, Dr. Carl Feltz, and he adjusted my spine, but it seemed like it only held for a couple of days, and I had to go back. I think I had to go back two or three times.

*****

Later, I remember watching DVDs with my wife in the bedroom. We watched old television shows. One of these old television shows was *The Beverly Hillbillies*. I remember having such a headache while we watched these shows.

*****

I also questioned my blood sugar as I had a history of hypoglycemia. The symptoms of hypoglycemia can mimic extreme symptoms of what I was experiencing, but I could not find an answer for what was wrong with me. I also remember that my water intake was low. I drank a gallon of water per day at the time, and I had not been drinking enough water. I went to work on January 7–9, 2019, but I noticed that my work efficiency was extremely low. I had

trouble focusing and concentrating. My headaches continued on these days.

*****

My second stroke was also a brain stem stroke. My second stroke occurred on January 23, 2019. I went and renewed my license plates for my truck and got a new driver's license prior to going to work at the jail. I remember trying to work on my computer. I had a relative who tried to get medication that he was no longer taking prior to seeing a doctor. He had threatened to turn me into the Mental Health Board if I did not get him the medication. The Mental Health Board incidentally had no authority over my actions, but they had the authority to prescribe psychotropic medication. The jail honored standing prescriptions but was stricter with psychotropic medication because a person could get high by taking it and would often request these medications for that reason, even if the prescription had expired years ago. My last official act on the job was to respond and send my relative a note that he was not being denied his medication, and that he had to have his appointment with the doctor. Since he was being threatening, I told him to turn me into the Mental Health

Board if he had to. To the best of my knowledge, he never filed a complaint.

I first noticed the second stroke after I lost my ability to write in my log. Before I told my supervisor, Lt. Tim Amstutz, about how I was feeling, I was ricocheting from one wall to another, trying to walk down the hall. We had a conversation, and he told me that I had been acting odd for about a month and that I should take a few days off to rest. He recommended that I go to the hospital and get checked out. He had one employee take me home, and another one took my truck to my home.

*****

When I got home, my wife was preparing to go to work at the bread store, where she was working at the time. So I asked my father to take me to St. Rita's Medical Center to the emergency department. Following a battery of tests, the doctor determined that I had had an ischemic stroke. Also, he discovered that I had had another ischemic stroke at an earlier date. This would have been the stroke that was misdiagnosed during my first visit. The St. Rita's Medical Center emergency doctor referred me to Dr. Osama Zaidat from St. Vincent's Hospital in Toledo, Ohio. St. Vincent's

Hospital was also in the Mercyhealth system with St. Rita's Medical Center.

*****

When I was transferred to St. Vincent's Hospital in Toledo, I was taken via ambulance.

There were two paramedics in the ambulance, and it was raining hard outside. The paramedics made the trip with their sirens on. I would be at St. Vincent Hospital from January 23, 2019, until February 6, 2019. I lost nineteen pounds during my stay. I eventually lost seventy-two pounds before Dr. Bowlus said I needed to stop losing weight.

I was admitted to St. Vincent's Hospital for facial weakness on the right side and slurred speech. Other reports added generalized weakness—especially on the right side— blurred vision, vertigo, loss of balance, poor coordination of walking, speech, and eye movements, and memory loss to my list of symptoms. Imagery also showed severe stenosis or narrowing of the basilar artery and an occluded or closed-up right distal vertebral artery. I had evidence of two strokes: one was a small cerebellar ischemic stroke, and the other stroke was a pontine ischemic stroke. One stroke was from my first trip to the hospital and was missed by the hospital staff. My second stroke occurred shortly before my second trip to the hospital.

When I arrived at St. Vincent's Hospital, I was taking atorvastatin 10 mg daily as needed. Statin medications help lower cholesterol. St. Vincent's Hospital put me on a heparin drip, which helps prevent blood clots. Simvastatin 80 mg daily, which helps treat high cholesterol, was also prescribed to me. I was given noninvasive ventilation, and I was designated a fall risk. On January 27, 2019, I was switched from a heparin drip and Plavix to Xarelto at 20 mg daily and aspirin at 81 mg daily. Plavix, Xarelto, and aspirin thin the blood.

When I arrived on the unit at St. Vincent's Hospital, I remember the nurses who were on duty transferring me from the ambulance gurney to a hospital bed. I would have the room to myself. I had not eaten since lunch, and I was extremely hungry. I remember eating two box lunches that the nurses had stored on the unit. Many times, the nurses were not able to feed me during the early part of my stay because I had to be ready for surgery at any time.

I remember that an MRI with contrast was done on my first night. My nurse took me through the hallways so fast that it felt like she had made the trip a hundred times. It was a long maze of hallways to me.

Dr. Zaidat and Dr. Bader Alenzi, completed an angiogram on January 24, 2019, to determine if my basilar artery could be cleaned out since it was almost completely blocked. They entered a catheter into my body through the femoral artery near the groin and advanced an X-ray to the basilar artery, which was blocked. The doctor left the intravascular sheath in place in case he had to clean the basilar artery. I was required to keep my leg as straight as I could for twenty-four hours. He eventually determined that it was too risky to clean out the blockage. I might die or enter a vegetative state. I remember that after the angiogram, I was asked if I had ever been a smoker because the artery was so small. I was told that it was as small as a pencil lead. I told the hospital staff that I had never been a smoker. During a later follow-up appointment with Dr. Mohamad Ezzeldin, I learned that my body created a new path in place of the basilar artery through which I get minimal blood flow. Because of this fact, I am still alive.

Blood work was taken at the hospital every day. Technicians drew blood a couple of times during the day and one time at night. After a few days, it became difficult to find a place in my arm to stick the needle. I always had an intravenous needle in my arm, whether I needed it or not. It was a hospital policy.

Since I was not able to get out of bed easily, I remained there most of the time. While in St. Vincent's Hospital, I had a multitude of doctors, and some of them were students. Throughout the day, many of them would check my neurological functions. They had me squeeze their fingers with my hands, follow their finger with my eyes, pull my toes toward myself as they held them back, rub the soles of my feet, and grin widely, showing my teeth. I soon knew the commands for the examination before the individual gave the commands.

I was also given several sponge baths by my nurses. This included a special cap with shampoo so I could wash my hair. I remember feeling uncomfortable when I was given a sponge bath because someone of the opposite sex usually had to give the sponge bath. I eventually got used to the idea of being given sponge baths by someone of the opposite sex because it seemed to be part of the routine for both hospitals where I stayed. The nurses also ensured as much privacy as they could.

One morning, I woke up to a loud alarm coming from my medical equipment. My BiPAP machine had developed an air leak somewhere. After what seemed like twenty minutes or so, help still had not come. The only thing I could think was that the alarm was not run all the way to the nurses' station, so no one heard it. I remember having to plug a tube with my finger and sleeping with it plugged to stop the alarm. Finally, a nurse came. I had to have at least four hours per night on the BiPAP, and I already had that amount of time. The nurse got my consent and just turned the BiPAP machine off.

Occasionally, I walked with a walker. It seemed like an extremely time-consuming task, and every step was a struggle. When I was completed, I had only walked a short distance. I did take more walks than what was required. I think that this was as much to relieve my boredom as anything else.

It seemed that I entertained myself with the television, even though my vision was blurry. I remember watching a lot of movies. It seemed like there was not much to do since I had to stay in bed. I slept a lot.

During my first weekend, I was evaluated by a physical therapist, an occupational therapist, and a speech therapist. I did very well on all my evaluations, and then I took a downward spiral by that Monday. A comment in some physical therapy notes confirmed the dates. It reported on Monday, January 28, 2019, that I reported not moving as well in physical therapy as when I was evaluated.

The National Institute on Aging states that for most stroke patients, rehabilitation mainly involves physical therapy. The aim of physical therapy is to have the stroke patient relearn simple motor activities, such as walking, sitting, standing, laying down, and the process of switching one type of movement to another. Another type of therapy to help patients relearn daily activities is occupational therapy. This type of therapy involves exercise and training. Its goal is to help a stroke patient relearn everyday activities, such as eating, drinking and swallowing, dressing, bathing, cooking, reading and writing, and using the toilet.

The National Institute on Aging states that speech therapy seeks to help the patient become independent or semi-independent. The National Institute on Aging states that speech therapy helps stroke patients relearn language and speaking skills or other forms of communication. Speech therapy is appropriate for patients who have no problem with cognition or thinking but have problems understanding speech or written words or problems forming speech. With time and patience, a stroke survivor should be able to regain some—and sometimes all—language and speaking ability.

Notes from my physical therapy report stated that I "used a rolling walker and took short/choppy steps." They report that I worked on "transferring in and out of shower, bed, the toilet, and from sitting to standing." I "walked 150 feet three times or one hundred feet twice." I tended to "walk to my right and ran into objects." They say that I was "cooperative and motivated to participate in physical therapy." I had to wear a gait belt, and several times, I had to walk on small sets of stairs with ten steps.

Notes from occupational therapy reported that I "needed minimal assistance with grooming but needed increased time to complete the task." I needed "a seated shower chair," and I "tended to have a left lean when standing." I had "some difficulty with eating." I also "needed standby assistance with bathing, dressing, and toileting."

I was not given speech therapy. I was assessed as having no apparent cognitive difficulties at the time of my evaluation. "No dysarthria or slurred speech was noted." Speech therapy was recommended, but notes indicate that I was only given verbal and written education.

Whenever I used the bathroom day or night, I used a urinal or a bedpan, which the nurse had to empty. This was a very difficult process.

I got many visitors, usually on the weekend. I had lots of visits from family and friends, but this was the first time I really became aware of how amazing my church family from Lima Community Church was. My pastor and his wife, Doug and Debbie Boquist, visited and sang Christian songs to me. I was also visited by members of my small group from church and by many other members of my congregation as well as a former small group member, who had moved away from Lima. I was surprised by these visits because I was so far from home at the time. I also was flooded with get-well cards, mostly from people at church.

My wife was able to stay with me in my room on weekends. The nurses allowed this because she was from out of town. One time, my wife was allowed to take me for a walk off the unit to other parts of the hospital. I had to go in a wheelchair, but the change of scenery was nice. I remember going to the gift shop and buying a card for the staff to thank them for all that they had done for me. I was also able to go through a historical display of the hospital on that walk.

*****

I remember having many conversations with people by text. I was usually slow when I texted because I was not very coordinated, but I passed a lot of time this way. I texted my wife every day. I also made many telephone calls. I remember talking with my brother, John Craft, about possibly retiring for the first time. At the time, I was not ready to retire.

When I did not have a visitor, I occupied myself by going for a walk with my walker with my nurse or with his/her aide. I also had many conversations with them about many things. I also practiced my writing. I usually practiced by printing the names of my chain of command at the sheriff's office. I remember my television being on late one night because I was having trouble sleeping, and I remember that I listened to Christian music on the television. I could not move, and I remember thinking that the rest of my life would be like this. I also remember having a lot of trouble seeing because my glasses were so old.

I remember one week that telephone calls became extremely important to me. We had wind chills of about fifty degrees below zero during the latter part of the winter of 2018–2019, so I did not have as many visitors because of the weather during my second week in Toledo. I missed the company. I remember calling my wife and telling her not to visit me that week because I did not want her to try to drive from Lima to Toledo in that kind of weather. Having no visitors was extremely difficult for me. I remember crying on the phone to my wife, Carol; father, Ronald Craft; and brother-in-law in Texas, John Kell. I remember crying to my wife and father for them to come and get me because I just wanted to go home. While it is possible that I was misreading the behavior of the nurses because of the strokes, it seemed like some of their comments were shaming in nature following my crying spells. My crying spells only lasted for several days so the comments seemed to go after several days too.

On January 29, 2019, I was transferred to a step-down unit of the hospital. I again had a room to myself. I began to help take care of self-care tasks after I was transferred to step-down. This was done under the supervision of an occupational therapist. My biggest problem was shaving. I was unsteady, and I nicked my face a lot. Since I was on a blood thinner, these nicks bled profusely. After several days, I had a lot of cuts on my face. I also needed monitoring when I took showers. Showers took longer because it seemed like I did not have any strength. I struggled to handle my bathing supplies while I used them, but I was able to clean myself independently during my showers.

The nurses let my wife stay for the weekend on this unit also because the distance from home was so great. The nurses let her sleep in my room, and she ate in the hospital cafeteria during one of her breaks. We talked a lot with each other and with the visitors that I received.

The hospital and my insurance company did not agree on what to do about additional treatment. My insurance company initially did not want additional treatment, and the hospital would not discharge me without it. I remember that I wanted to go outside without a coat and freeze myself to death if the two could not come to an agreement. I did not tell my wife of these thoughts until much later. I remember one of the two of them finally suggesting Flower Hospital in Sylvania, Ohio, as an option, but I wanted something closer to home. Finally, my insurance company agreed to Lima Manor Nursing Home in Lima, Ohio, because it was in the network. They approved ten days for additional treatment.

I remember that on the day I was discharged, I watched several Westerns while I waited. I also watched a documentary on the development of warfarin, which was once used as rat poison but is now used as a blood thinner.

At discharge, I was prescribed Xarelto 20 mg daily, aspirin 81 mg daily, and Simvastatin 80 mg daily. Xarelto and aspirin were blood thinners. Simvastatin was for cholesterol. I was taken by an ambulance for transfer to Lima Manor Nursing Home in Lima, Ohio.

CHAPTER 2

I returned to Lima again in an ambulance. I was heading to Lima Manor Nursing Home. It was overcast and drizzling. It seemed like the ride took forever, but at least, I would be close to home, and people could visit me even in bad weather!

*****

When I arrived at Lima Manor Nursing Home, I was taken to a small room that was large enough for two people to live in. It was a room reserved for treatment patients instead of long-term care patients. According to my physical at Lima Manor Nursing Home, I had mild, right-sided weakness and facial weakness.

The lobby of Lima Manor Nursing Home had an enclosure for small birds. Looking at the birds was for the enjoyment of residents.

I was there during the winter months, so smoking was more restricted for those residents who did smoke. There were prescribed intervals that residents could use a designated outdoor smoking area. There was no smoking inside the facility. Smoking is a habit that I never formed; however, my wife's Uncle Dennis, who was a long-term resident, made frequent use of the smoking area.

I initially did not have a roommate, but I was eventually given a roommate for a short time. He had slipped on the ice while trying to leave the hospital from another procedure and had broken some bones. He was in a lot of pain and moaned frequently. One night, he moaned continuously, and third-shift staff moved me down the hall to another room.

I woke early every morning and gave myself a sponge bath. I took a sponge bath in my sink almost daily. I was offered a shower twice during the ten days that I was a resident. Taking a sponge bath was still a long and difficult task, but I was able to wash myself independently. I still nicked myself shaving a lot, and I had lots of cuts on my face.

Lima Manor Nursing Home had laundry facilities, but my wife took my clothes home to wash, and she gave me clean ones. The drawers that a resident had were small, so you could only have a few outfits.

I usually ate lunch in my room, but I ate breakfast and supper in the dining room. When a person ate, the staff would serve them a tray with the meal which had already been selected the day before. Breakfast time seemed like the social hour for residents. I usually ate breakfast with my wife's Uncle Dennis. I often ate dinner with my wife and one or two of my stepchildren. Lima Manor encouraged families to have meals with residents, and fortunately, my wife visited me almost daily. I remember one day that Seth, Selah, and Melody also visited with my wife. It had been about a month since I had seen my stepchildren.

I also received a lot of visits from my parents, Ronald and Carol Craft, and siblings and spouse, Christyn Craft, and John and Dawn Craft. My parents eventually made their annual trip to Florida, so they could only come and visit during the first part of my stay. My brother was the maintenance supervisor of a nursing home in St. Mary's, Ohio, as well as a captain with the Lima Fire Department. His wife was the director of nursing at the same nursing home where he worked as a maintenance supervisor. It was run by the same corporation that ran Lima Manor Nursing Home. I also remember my sister, Christyn, visiting me at that time. My wife's aunt, Carolyn Werner, surprised me and bought a Valentine's card and gift for me to give to Carol. I do not know how I would have given my wife anything that year if her aunt had not been so thoughtful.

I also got a number of visitors from the sheriff's office. I was surprised by a group of coworkers, including an intern, who had started running my office in my absence. At this point, my coworkers and I still expected me to return to work after recuperating from the two strokes.

I continued to be amazed at how many people visited me from church. One of the people who visited me from church was Don McClure. He and his wife, Pam, were also extremely helpful to Carol and the kids. Since we got water from a well at that point, my family drank water that they got from a local water company. Don and his wife helped them get water as well as milk and other items.

I was in treatment for the second time at Lima Manor. My treatment regimen consisted of physical therapy, occupational therapy, and speech therapy. In physical therapy, I remember practicing with my walker. The physical therapists had me use my walker a lot in the hallways. I also remember being on a machine with weights to strengthen my legs. I also remember doing a lot of ring tosses while I was there. In occupational therapy, I did some cooking. I also practiced on a pedaling machine to strengthen my legs. In speech therapy, I learned about keeping a list of things that I did not want to forget. I still keep lists of items that I do not want to forget on my cell phone. I also learned how to set up medications by putting beads, rather than pills, in medication containers. I also completed cognitive tasks in speech therapy.

I had most of my treatment before lunch, so the rest of the day I could spend as I pleased. I remember playing bingo and doing activities with other residents. I remember on one occasion that a woman had a church service that I attended. One day, I won five games of bingo. I won a dime for each game. When I was through playing, I was able to buy a can of soda pop.

I spent a lot of time watching television. I remember one day that the History Channel ran a marathon of episodes from a series about people who believed there were extraterrestrials. I personally do not believe in extraterrestrials and thought that the believers on the show were making great leaps in logic.

On one occasion, I remember borrowing a book from another patient's sister-in-law. She was related to the Sarber family. Sheriff Jesse Sarber had been shot and killed while serving as sheriff of Allen County, Ohio, and I had written *The Sheriffs of Allen County, Ohio: 1831 through 2017* about a year earlier, so the book about the Sarber family was extremely interesting to me.

One day, I went to a conference room and met with my wife and some of my therapists. The staff told me that they were going to recommend that my insurance company extend my treatment and approve more days in the nursing home. My insurance company ignored Lima Manor staff's recommendation to extend my treatment. The insurance company notified Lima Manor late in the afternoon on a Friday that they were not going to authorize an extension, so I was released on a Saturday afternoon without a plan. Following the release, I needed to return to Lima Manor to be assessed by Dr. James Bowlus, my family doctor, in order to continue my Family and Medical Leave Act. He visited me for this purpose, but he was unaware that I had just been released. At least, I did not have to go to his office for an appointment to fill out the paperwork.

*****

My wife tried to convince my insurance company to pay for outpatient treatment by Lima Manor Nursing Home staff. I was assessed by Lima Manor staff, but shortly after my insurance company had approved the outpatient treatment, I had to go back to St. Rita's Medical Center for my third and fourth strokes. The two strokes happened within days of each other.

I remember having a bad headache and going to see Melody compete in the Allen County, Ohio, spelling bee on a Saturday morning. This headache was undoubtedly due to a stroke, but my wife and I thought that it was the residual effects of my first and second strokes, so we did not seek help immediately. The first of these two strokes happened the day after a follow-up appointment in Toledo, Ohio. We had gone to the theater in Bluffton, Ohio, that night after the appointment.

My wife and I were preparing a new low-sodium recipe for Cornish hens to entertain my mother-in-law, Eva Bowen, and my wife's aunt, Carolyn Werner. I had an extremely bad headache that afternoon during the preparation of the meal. I found that it was much harder to get around with my walker after the headache. This was likely also from a stroke.

I believe that my dog knew I was going to have my fourth stroke. I got out of the van in the garage after what I think was my third stroke and before my fourth stroke. My dog barked uncontrollably at me. It seemed like she was barking urgently and was not afraid. I had never heard her bark like that before, but I ignored her at the time.

CHAPTER 3

About two weeks after I left Lima Manor Nursing Home, I had my third and fourth strokes. They were also brain stem strokes. One of the strokes occurred on the left side of the pons, and the other occurred on the right posterior pons. Like my first and second strokes, there is no way to know which stroke occurred first. They probably occurred on February 23, 2019, and February 27, 2019.

*****

During that time, I made a telephone call to my brother, John Craft, on February 28, 2019, to see if he could take me to an optometrist in the next couple of days. He was a firefighter with the rank of captain with the Lima Fire Department and was on his way to his part-time job as a maintenance supervisor at a nursing home in Celina, Ohio. He was going there to pick up his wife, Dawn Craft, who also worked there as the director of nursing. My brother handed the phone to Dawn while he drove, and she started talking to me. She then asked if anyone was home to help me get ready because they were changing the route to come and get me to take me to St. Rita's Medical Center to make sure that I did not have another stroke. Carol was at work, so my stepdaughter, Melody Gallaspie, helped me get ready. Melody later reported that my left eye was twitching, and my right eye was motionless. I could barely make it to my brother's car with my walker, but we finally made it to the emergency room of St. Rita's Medical Center. The trip to the hospital was a blur.

*****

My church's hospital visitation pastor, Terry Ayers, was already in the emergency room for another individual, so he prayed for me also and notified the pastor of Lima Community Church, Doug Boquist.

I shared my complaints of double vision (diplopia) and tingling or a prickling sensation in the left arm and hand (paresthesia). The diplopia started one week before admission and resolved itself and then returned on the day of admission. I had expressive aphasia that started at noon on the day of admission. I had some difficulty speaking certain words and completing thoughts.

The emergency room staff conducted a few tests and then sent me to 4A Neuroscience. I remember on my first night that I felt like I was hanging upside down to sleep. The next morning, on March 1, 2019, I had an MRI which confirmed my third and fourth strokes. I was asked to read a calendar. The number "1" was three inches high on the calendar, but it appeared slightly blurry to me.

On March 18, 2019, I also reported left-hand numbness. It was related to my strokes.

While on 4A, I remember that one morning, a physical therapist or occupational therapist worked with me, exercising with TheraBands and trying to toss balls into a basket.

The nursing staff also gave me an eye patch because I had double vision. I remember crying because my vision was so bad. My aunt, Mary Grosvenor, had double vision after having seven hemorrhagic strokes five years earlier. I wondered how I was going to make it at least five years with vision this bad.

I had a conversation with my sister-in-law, Dawn Craft, while I was on 4A. One of the questions she asked me was if I had any Aflac policies. I remembered that I had a policy for catastrophic injuries and strokes. I bought the policy before I had gotten married, so I had forgotten about it. I told my wife about it during a phone call that night, and she started the process of collecting on the policy. Aflac handled the claim quickly.

After the weekend, I spoke to Dr. Donald Arthur, who was the doctor who ran 7E Rehabilitation, about completing rehabilitation at St. Rita's Medical Center for my two new strokes. I was excited about the possibility of treatment on 7E Rehabilitation, but we had to get the approval of the insurance company for the services. The insurance company had just approved outpatient treatment at Lima Manor Nursing Home, and now, I had a new request to make. Had I participated in outpatient treatment at Lima Manor Nursing Home, the program would have been my third time in a treatment program. Fortunately, the insurance company approved the decision to go through the treatment at St. Rita's Medical Center without stalling. Soon after, I transferred to 7E for rehabilitation on March 4, 2019. I started treatment for the third time the next day.

My Xarelto and Simvastatin were discontinued, and I started taking Eliquis 5 mg twice daily and Atorvastatin 40 mg once daily. The Eliquis was a blood thinner, and the Atorvastatin was for cholesterol.

I found out that prism glasses might help with my double vision. The hospital worked with Dr. Teresa Rohrs in Ottawa, Ohio, regarding stroke patients with double vision. My insurance company would consider it checking out of the hospital against medical advice if I went to see Dr. Rohrs before I completed treatment. If this happened, then they would not be obligated to pay for further services. I decided to live with extremely blurry, double vision for the month in which I participated in treatment. Then I went to the optometrist on April 4, 2019.

In addition to my extremely blurry, double vision, I was terribly weak, and my balance was poor. I was forgetful, and my speech was slurred. I also found that it was even more difficult to get around with my walker. I fully expected to die, so I planned my own funeral so that Carol would not have that burden. I remember that the one hymn I wanted to be played was "Jesus Christ is Risen Today." I did not care what other music the funeral home played. As of the publication of this book, I have heard some arrangements of this song for four Easters in a row. It is always quite an emotional experience for me when this hymn is played.

The room that I was assigned on 7E had a helipad just outside. At first, this was not a problem, but it became a nuisance in the middle of the night when I was trying to sleep through the noise.

I usually took some kind of sponge bath every day. If it was a day that I took a full sponge bath, I had to ensure that I had my wife move my bathing supplies, if necessary, to a shelf that I could reach. One shelf was difficult to reach from a sitting position. An occupational therapist supervised me when I was given a shower every other day. On those days, I at least washed my hair during the sponge bath. During the shower, I still had to bathe in front of a female, which was embarrassing. But they tried to ensure your privacy. I washed myself while sitting in a shower chair. I still found it difficult to shave in the morning because I still nicked myself, and it still bled. Finally, I had my wife buy me an electric razor. This solved the problem.

The night shift seemed much more relaxed than the day shift. When the night shift came on duty, treatment had already been completed for the day, and the rest of the hustle and bustle of the day was over. I wheeled around the unit in my wheelchair for long periods of time. Sometimes, I wheeled around several times before my wife came and after she left. I was the only patient who did this. I did it to build up my strength as well as pass the time.

I also did sit-ups in my bed in the early morning to strengthen myself. I had trouble doing ten sit-ups when I started, but I eventually raised the number up to between twenty-five to thirty sit-ups.

I worked on a lot of word search puzzles while I was in the hospital. I have always liked word search puzzles. Kellie Saine, RT, and her intern kept me supplied with plenty of word search puzzles. She also left the patients jigsaw puzzles to work on. I stopped and put pieces of the puzzles in place when I wheeled around in my wheelchair.

I always rearranged the table and other furniture in my room when I got up in the morning and before I went to bed at night. I moved the extra chairs so that they were between the bed and the window at night. I moved them out during the day so they could be used. This was difficult to do from a sitting position in a wheelchair without setting off an alarm. I always tried to move the furniture in the morning after my sponge bath before the alarm on my wheelchair was hooked back up for the day.

I also wrote sentences to practice my writing. I wrote, "I will beat the strokes."

At night, I usually voided in a portable urinal, and the nurse emptied it. If I needed to take a bowel movement, I called the nurse because my bed was set with an alarm to sense movement. I then transferred to my walker and walked across the room. I then transferred to the toilet.

During the day, I had to use the toilet with the help of a nurse or a nurse's aide. That person had to help transfer me to the toilet.

Whenever I needed to transfer from my wheelchair to my recliner or my bed, the nurse had to put a gait belt on me. This was for my safety.

My course of treatment would include physical therapy, occupational therapy, and speech therapy. This was the third time I was in treatment. In physical therapy, I was assessed for the strength in my right lower extremities and my left lower extremities. I was assessed "within functional limits" for both. I was assessed as "scooting for bed mobility." Standby assistance was recommended. I needed "contact guard assistance or one to two hands on body for transfers." I was assessed for sit to stand and stand to sit. I was also assessed for "ambulation on a surface of level tile." I "used a rolling walker, and my quality of gait was slightly unsteady, minimally ataxic unsteady, staggering with foot placement, discontinuous steps. I needed cues to stay close to the walker especially with turns." I had "no major loss of balance, and I was tested for a distance of forty feet."

During physical therapy, I walked with my walker a lot. I also did exercises on a balance beam and also on an exercise table. I also walked through cones, did ring toss, and tried to get baskets by throwing a ball into a basket. I remember that my very first treatment session was in physical therapy with Cathy Kirakofe, PT. I ambulated all over the unit with my walker. She had the attitude of *"when* I get better rather than *if* I get better." I found that the therapists in all three disciplines had this attitude. One issue that I had later on in physical therapy was easily corrected with another pair of shoes. My old pair of shoes no longer provided proper support.

In occupational therapy, I was assessed as needing contact guard assistance when assessed for "dressing, bed mobility, transfers, and balance." During occupational therapy, I continued to work on stretching TheraBands. I also learned cooking, cleaning, and laundry skills. I also worked on strengthening my eyes due to double vision with Jamie Dickman, OT. Jamie had me work on exercises to focus my eyes as well as exercises to make them stronger. I worked on tasks to test the strength of my hands. Furthermore, I worked on various other tasks and problem-solving skills with my hands.

In my final week or so, I walked over to the outpatient rehabilitation facilities and worked on a Dynavision to help me prepare for the computerized driving test. I responded to lights on a wall by hitting them when they lit up. This measured my reaction time. A certain score was necessary on this exercise before a person could take the computerized driving test while he/she was in outpatient therapy. Shortly before I was discharged, Carol and I spent a night in the functional apartment. This helped reveal problems that we might encounter at home. Couples could prepare meals in the apartment or order out to have their meals delivered by the hospital cafeteria. We chose to order our meals from the cafeteria.

In speech therapy, my assessment reported that I "had excellent insight into my vision deficits, expressing to the speech therapist that I had discovered ways to compensate (i.e., closing one eye)." The assessment stated that I "had slight difficulty with delayed recall, though I was aware of the difficulty." It reported that I had "adequate conversational discourse and receptive and expressive language skills intact." I reported that I "had previously received speech therapy at Lima Manor Skilled Nursing Facility, and I was requesting continued inpatient services. Speech therapy provided education regarding good cognitive performance and options for continued speech therapy if desired." I expressed understanding. The report recommended "continued speech therapy targeting recall and overall compensation for difficulties secondary to visual deficits per my request." In speech therapy, I continued working on setting up the medication with beads rather than pills. I practiced memorizing lists of items. I also worked on problem-solving and cognitive skills by completing various exercises.

Our common area which was used for treatment was built like a little town. It contained a car, a gas pump, a gardening store, a small market, an Arby's, a chapel, a mailbox, a newspaper stand, and a functional apartment.

Offices also were designed to look like store fronts for a bank, an employment agency, a mechanical services company, a travel agency, an insurance company, an attorney's office, and a real estate agency.

During this time, I was also extremely fearful of death. I was extremely weak and expected to die at any time. One day, a visitor had left a prayer square for me that she had picked up at a nurses' station. It had been knitted for the hospital by a volunteer. It had also been prayed over. I remember on that night, my nurse was helping me to bed. My vision was still extremely bad, so the nurse explained to me that the blurry light blue piece of cloth on my night-stand was a prayer square that someone had left for me. The attached scripture was from John 16:33. She then read it to me: "*These things I have spoken to you, so that you may have peace. In the world you have tribulation, but take courage; I have overcome the world.*" That night, I became extremely frightened that I would die in my sleep. I kept catching myself starting to doze and woke with a start. I gasped for air as I woke up. Sometime during my fright, I looked over at my prayer square and realized that I could see it more clearly. I also realized that I could also read the scripture more clearly. I began to cry and read the scripture over and over. I knew God was telling me that I was not going to die that night.

I also remember having to stay in my seat in my room at all times unless I was in therapy so I would not fall down. My wheelchair had an alarm on it, which I accidentally set off several times. Nurses and all other available staff came running from everywhere when I did this. I usually stayed in my wheelchair after treatment sessions because I had more mobility in my wheelchair than in my recliner.

Dr. Arthur made rounds almost daily. He was very intelligent, and I had been told that he was an engineer before studying for his medical degree. If I asked him a question, he gave me an extremely detailed answer. I always liked that about him. I remember talking to him about my BiPAP machine. I knew that it recorded brain waves and transmitted them on the Internet to Jennifer Jacobs. I thought that this machine had recorded the four strokes that I had had up to this time. He told me that he did not think that the BiPAP machine could make sense of my strokes, but he called to make sure. He found out that the BiPAP machine was able to read the strokes as an anomaly but could not pick up any details of my strokes.

One time during my stay, I had a Transient Ischemic Attack (TIA). I was wheeling out of my room for a physical therapy session, and I went limp for several seconds, and my tongue swelled briefly. My speech was slurred slightly when I tried to explain what had happened. I was in my wheelchair, so the staff member rolled me down to the nurses' station. Dr. Arthur was there, and after an examination, he said that I might have had a TIA. Since I was tired after this event, the staff member canceled my treatment session for that day and let me lay down for a while. A note in my hospital paperwork noted that on March 22, 2019, I had an "episode of onset of dysarthria (difficult or unclear articulation of speech that is otherwise linguistically normal) with 'tongue swelling' with impression of TIA from hypotension (BP 117/54) versus restart of ACE-I."

During one of my physical therapy sessions, the staff filmed me walking with my walker. They asked if they could record this for hospital public relations. It was never used for advertising, but I figured it also served as a good photographic record of my progress.

Since I was worried about what I would be able to do when I returned to work, Dr. Arthur referred me for a neuropsychological examination. Since this referral had to be made about six weeks in advance, Dr. Arthur made the referral while I was still a patient at the hospital, with the testing to occur after I was released as a patient. A note in my hospital records on March 15, 2019, showed that the appointment had been made with Dr. Timothy Wynkoop. This examination would be conducted in Maumee, Ohio, on April 25, 2019. It consisted of a number of psychological tests that recorded an extremely accurate record of where I was intellectually, emotionally, and functionally. The examination took most of the day to complete. My wife and I traveled to Maumee the night before the examination and stayed with Irma Ayers, a former member of my church small group, who had moved away from Lima and had also come to visit me in St. Vincent's Hospital in Toledo.

I remember that I was visited several times by the unit manager, Amy Bok, RN, MSN, CRRN. She wanted to check to make sure that the staff were doing a good job and whether I needed anything.

Although patients were free to eat meals in their own rooms, we were encouraged to eat lunch on weekdays with other patients in the Arby's room. Some patients chose not to participate and ate in their rooms, but those of us who did eat lunch together grew a lot closer to each other. Also, family members were allowed to bring lunch and eat with the group. Carol joined us several times. Carol and I became close to a lady who had been a patient for a number of months. She had almost died from a diabetic coma and had been staying in 7E Rehabilitation. My wife found a simple recipe for a sugar-free chocolate frosty on the Internet. Occupational therapists let me make it for her during a treatment session and then surprise her with it at lunch.

While I was in the hospital, I became extremely familiar with communicating with the outside world through Facebook and texting. My vision did become a little clearer, but unfortunately, I did not learn that you could enlarge text on a phone until after I had been discharged.

We were visited occasionally by volunteer pet therapists. One day, we had a pet therapist come in, and the dog handler worked in communications at the sheriff's office. It was nice to catch up on what was happening at the office with a coworker.

I received a lot of visits from families and friends. One visitor that I remember, Terry Hunt, also volunteered as a chaplain at the jail. We had worked together providing interventions with the Western Ohio Critical Incident Stress Management Team. He was also in charge of the 46.1 Response Ohio Team with the Assemblies of God Church. It was always good to see him.

I also remember two twin brothers from church who visited quite often, Dean and Dale Henderson. Dale had suffered a stroke about thirty-eight years previously and functioned fairly normally. I knew him, but I did not know of his stroke until after I had my fourth stroke. His survival was big news to me. It was comforting to know that someone had survived for thirty-eight years and was living a normal life.

I also remember on one occasion that members of the men's prayer group came and visited. They prayed and anointed me. It was an extremely emotional visit. I remember being overcome by emotion as they did this. I also received many visits from members of the pastoral staff at my church. I remember that Doug Boquist, our lead pastor; Brad Taylor, our executive pastor; and Philip Starr, our youth pastor made many visits. They brought me a lot of hope, and I did not feel so abandoned.

Bill Harthun, a friend from church, whom I used to work with at the jail, visited me several times. We had become extremely close working together in the jail. One day, he brought me a hamburger from Kewpee, a local hamburger restaurant chain. It was a welcome change from hospital food for every meal.

My favorite visits were from my wife. She came almost every day, usually in the evening. We were able to leave the unit later in my stay, but I had to stay in my wheelchair. We usually stayed inside the hospital on most days because it was still cool outside. We went to the hospital chapel a lot. We had many deep talks during those times because we both knew that there was still a chance that I could die.

Another thing that was important to me was that my small group from church started meeting weekly at the hospital. We started meeting in my room, but the hospital staff allowed us to meet in the Arby's room so we would have more room to meet. I remember a couple of meetings where I became extremely tearful talking about what was happening.

People from church also were extremely supportive of Carol and the kids. The church started a food train in which a different family provided Carol and the kids with an evening meal every day so Carol did not have to prepare meals and could spend more time at the hospital. They continued this for a short time after I was discharged.

*****

Toward the end of my hospital stay, I set three goals for myself to guide my recovery. They were:

(1) Find your new normal and go for it.
(2) Pay attention to detail.
(3) Never give up, ever.

I was already guiding myself by these principles, but after I put them into words, I made the decision to put more emphasis on them in the future. These goals really helped me during my stay.

I also signed a medical power of attorney while I was in the hospital. I did this so my wife could make decisions for me if anything should happen to me. I signed this after a hospital chaplain talked to the two of us about it.

Social Worker Day also occurred while I was in the hospital. I remember hospital staff putting a sign on my door because I was a social worker. It was nice that the hospital staff remembered these things in such detail.

I also visited a meeting of what was known as the Stroke Club at that time. It was a support group that we could attend after discharge. I do not remember a lot about the meeting because of my strokes. I do remember seeing a nurse—whose identity I did not remember—who introduced herself as a nurse who had cared for me while I was still a patient on 4A Neuroscience.

As my hospital stay was coming to an end, I first had the idea of volunteering at the hospital on 7E after I had a little bit of success with my recovery from my strokes. This later became a reality for me.

My time on 7E was extremely successful. I had made a lot of progress. I remember having Carol bring me a lot of thank you cards. I wrote them a few at a time because it was still difficult to write because of my strokes. I kept them all in a drawer and passed them all out at once after I had finished writing them.

Finally, Carol and I were able to spend the night in the functional apartment. We ordered our meals from the hospital cafeteria. I was not feeling really well, but the stay in the apartment went well. My shower in the morning was a little different for me. There was a hard plastic bench in the tub. Half of the bench fit in the tub while half of it was outside of the tub. I was able to sit on the bench, while I was outside of the tub and then slide over the tub to take a shower. It was also nice not to have to wish Carol farewell at the end of the night for once.

Following our stay in the apartment, I soon was finished with treatment, and I was wheeled down the hall to the nurses' station and was able to take part in the tradition of ringing the bell, which indicated that a patient's treatment was completed successfully. This was a happy time for me.

CHAPTER 4

I was released from the hospital on March 29, 2019. When I arrived home from the hospital, I found that my wife had had Bill Harthun, our friend from church, install grab bars in my restroom so that I would not fall down. My wife had even removed the rugs so I would not trip over them. My shower had a stool to use for a shower chair. While I was always independent while using the shower, my wife did not want me to shower unless she was in the house because she was afraid I would fall and hurt myself. I never had any problems showering, so when she was comfortable that I would not fall, I was able to shower with no one being at home.

I also had to enter the house through the garage because I had not regained my balance, and the door from the garage to the house had a hand rail. When I went to a small group from church, I also entered the Burky house—where the study was held—from the garage for the same reason. I would enter both houses from the garage for some time until I had improved my balance.

I had a porta potty set up in my bedroom at night, but I never used it. Initially, I transferred from my bed to my wheelchair. I rolled across the bedroom to the bathroom door. I then transferred to my walker at the bathroom door and used the toilet. As I became more independent, I walked to the bathroom with my walker in order to use the toilet. When I became independent enough that I was able to walk, I just walked. I had a night light to use at night.

During the day, I used my wheelchair or walker to get to the bathroom. If I was in a wheelchair, I transferred from my wheelchair to the walker and then to the toilet. When I became independent enough to walk, I simply walked to the bathroom as I needed.

I also stayed on the hospital schedule after I got home, and I went to bed early. I did this to help alleviate any compassion fatigue that my wife may develop in caring for me. This gave her a couple of hours each night to watch a movie or to spend time with her children.

Our dog seemed extremely happy that I was home. When I tried to read on the back patio, she always came over and checked on me. Our cat was more likely to stand off from me. It seemed like he did not remember who I was at first. After he seemed to remember me, he would wrap around my ankles. This was a problem until I stepped on him a couple of times.

When I got home from the hospital, Carol asked me to wear lounge pants and other loose-fitting clothing to help with my blood flow. Carol had read on the Internet that loose-fitting clothing would help with my blood flow. I wore loose-fitting clothing for about six months.

The weekend after my release from the hospital, I used my cell phone by placing it inside a three-dimensional viewer. I found that with one of the apps on my cell phone and the lenses on the viewer, my double vision was corrected, and I could see fairly clearly. I used this three-dimensional program and other programs like it until I got a new cell phone that was longer than the viewer. It was nice to be able to slip into my own little world where I was able to see clearly again.

*****

I had to see a number of specialists that summer, and Carol had enlisted a group of men to help her transport me to see them. My wife had enlisted Bill Harthun and Don McClure from church to help transport me to my appointments. She also enlisted Hal Shields, my uncle, to help.

*****

On April 3, 2019, I was evaluated for the St. Rita's Medical Center Outpatient Treatment Program. It was my fourth time through treatment. I was assessed for physical therapy, occupational therapy, and speech therapy. I went to therapy twice per week, and my last day was on July 1, 2019. Sometimes, Carol or one of the men who helped with transport would take me. Other times, I was transported through Mercy Transport or Black & White Cab Company, which was contracted through Mercy Transport and operated by St. Rita's Medical Center.

In physical therapy, my short-term goals were as follows:

1) Improve balance with a Tinetti score of 20/28 or greater to assist with ambulation at home
2) Improve LE (lower extremities) to 5/5 to assist with stability walking on steps
3) Improve ambulation with the patient by walking with a straight cane at an improved pace and good heel strike to assist with community outings
4) Patient able to ascend/descend four steps using reciprocal pattern and bilateral handrails to assist with going in and out of the house

My long-term goal was to be independent with HEP (home exercise program) and with progression to assist with decreasing pain.

Some of my exercises were as follows:

1) Walk with a cane
2) NuStep machine
3) Rocker board for support and balance
4) Hydro hip machine
5) Three-way hip exercises
6) Heel/toe raises, marching, squats on foam
7) Balance on foam
8) Heel-to-toe ambulation forward and retro
9) Hydro stick for balance
10) Hydro chest for abduction bracing
11) NK (Noland and Kuckho) table for flexion and extension

Physical therapists reported at a case conference on May 2, 2019, that I was "doing well with PT Cane trial last session but requires minimum and moderate cues. Recommend continued ambulation with walker. Five visits in the clinic for strength and balance in the sessions. Tinetti 17/28 in the evaluation and LE (lower extremities) strength 4 + 5."

In occupational therapy, 1) "I used right upper extremities to reach and turn/place tile on tile board on wall; 2) Spread coins out on left side of table and patient had to use left hand to pick them up; 3) O'Connor dexterity task just using fingers to pick up pegs with bilateral hands; 4) Patient used right hand to flip discs over to red from midline all the way to the left of the board to facilitate left side attention and fine motor skills, then use left hand to turn discs back to yellow from left side to midline."

I also used the Dynavision to prepare for the driving test.

Occupational therapists reported at a case conference on May 2, 2019: "During his time in the clinic, focused on low vision deficits, weight bearing and coordination of RUE (right upper extremities). Patient very motivated. Moderate difficulty with RUE (right upper extremities) fine motor coordination activity. During reading activity, noting that he is missing letters on both the right and left side of the line of text and skips lines of text without awareness. Plan to continue to address vision and physical deficits. Returns to optometrist on 5/19/19."

In speech therapy, my short-term goals were as follows:

1) Patient will complete working memory/manipulation tasks with no more than minimal cues, eighty

percent of the time for improved success with work-related tasks

2) Assess complex attention, and add goals as indicated

3) Assess high-level organization/scheduling, and add goals as indicated

4) Patient will complete high-level thought organizations and scheduling tasks with modified interventions seventy-five percent of the time for improved success with job-related duties and daily tasks

Some of the interventions used in speech therapy are as follows:

1) Divided attention assessed via circling odd numbers throughout the stimulus sheet while verbalizing the category given three items presented auditorily. Zero errors with the written part of the task and zero errors (13/13 categories) with the auditory part of the task

2) Patient utilized a paper to help with visual tracking from one line to the next with good success

3) Patient completed a scheduling task given, seven tasks to be completed, and details about when the

tasks will be completed provided in a paragraph format

The speech therapist reports that "he feels his vision is better. Addressing working memory: good improvements noted. Addressing higher level thought organization and scheduling. Overall, does well, minimal cues provided, required. Patient feels that a lot of his errors are due to his low vision. He has to return to work in August. Reports that he will lose everything if he does not return to work."

While at home, I also wrote a couple of exercises for speech therapy. I mailed copies to Dana Diller, SLP, my inpatient speech therapist.

*****

On April 4, 2019, I went to see Dr. Teresa Rohrs, in Ottawa, Ohio, for the first of several visits to be tested for prism glasses to help with my double vision. One day, I went to lunch with my wife, and afterward, we went to pick up my new prism glasses. It was a surprise for me that we were going to get my glasses. Don McClure had transported me to my first appointment with Dr. Rohrs and then to another appointment in which I was examined a second time for any changes to my vision. I also ordered glasses during that visit. I remember that I cried after I put on my new glasses because I could see clearly for the first time in months. I believe some of Dr. Rohrs' staff cried also because of how I reacted. I looked at the countryside on the way home. I could not believe how clear it was. I had to cease going to see Dr. Rohrs because I had the wrong type of Medicaid. When I went on it, she was not on the provider list.

*****

On May 1, 2019, and May 16, 2019, I went to see Dr. Ewa Mrozek. I had blood testing to see if I had any factors that would cause my blood to clot for any reason. I was tested for numerous clotting factors, but I did not have any of them.

*****

Dr. Bowlus referred me to a heart specialist for a checkup. I saw Dr. Kishore Nallu in his office. Although my heart was not in perfect shape, it was in good enough shape that I did not have to see a heart specialist on a regular basis.

*****

Next, I had my initial consultation with Dr. Ali Almudallal, a neurologist; and Paige Leopold, CNP, his assistant on April 24, 2019. He ordered a Magnetic Resonance Image (MRI) that was taken on June 6, 2019. My follow-up appointment was on the day after the MRI. Dr. Almudallal told me that my condition was getting worse and that I was going to have a fifth stroke and die. This was extremely upsetting to both Carol and me. We began searching the Internet for anything. I texted the news to my pastor, Doug Boquist, who was extremely supportive.

*****

I went out of town for the weekend for the wedding of my wife's cousin. At the wedding reception, it was difficult thinking of Selah and Melody, my two stepdaughters who were also at the wedding, getting married in the future and me not being alive for the ceremony. My wife told me that she would never marry again because if I died, she would have lost two husbands before all of her kids graduated from high school, and she did not want the pain of possibly losing a third husband.

*****

When we got back home, we found out that my church had prayed over a member of the congregation that weekend who was standing in my place for me. It was good to know that I had their prayers and concern.

*****

Several weeks later, Carol and I visited the church of the pastor who married us. His congregation also prayed for me not to have a fifth stroke and die.

*****

On October 16, 2019, I had another sleep study to see if I still needed to stay on my BiPAP machine because I had lost so much weight since I had been in the hospital. They found that I had improved but not enough to go off the BiPAP machine.

*****

When I started walking, I walked along the edge of my bed. If I fell, I would fall on my mattress. I did this a lot when my wife was at work and my stepchildren were at school because no one, including my physical therapists from outpatient therapy, thought that it was safe for me to try to walk, and I did not want anyone to know that I was trying.

When someone was at home, I stayed in my wheelchair or used my walker. It was inconvenient to use my wheelchair because the doorway to my bedroom was not very wide, and it was difficult to roll my wheelchair through. There are scrape marks on my doorposts from trying to maneuver my wheelchair through the door. Finally, my outpatient physical therapists relented and let me walk with a cane.

I walked with a cane on Mother's Day. I remember walking a mile in my hallway using a cane. I used pennies to keep track of how many laps I walked. I did not hurt much from walking, but when I did, I kept walking anyway. I quickly realized that I would have to move my walking outside to keep it interesting. Carol did not want me to walk on the road because there was heavy traffic, and walking would be too dangerous. I asked our neighbors if I could walk on a paved lane on their property so I would not have to walk on the road. The neighbors gladly let me walk in their lane. The distance was eight round trips on the lane to walk a mile. I usually walked between one mile and 3.1 miles or five kilometers. I also walked at the Lima Mall and at Lima Community Church, which was about a mile away. I used a cane when walking most of the summer, but by the middle of the summer, I was able to walk independently again.

One day, while I was walking, I came up with the idea of walking the Allen County Sheriff's Office National Night Out 5K Run/Walk in August 2019. I decided to walk this 5K because it was staffed by my former coworkers, and they were all familiar with my medical condition. I reasoned that if the 5K went poorly, they would know enough to take me to the hospital immediately, and they would have cruisers with lights and sirens to get me to the hospital quickly. I practiced walking almost daily so that I would do well walking the 5K. I found out that I am able to walk much faster in competition than in practice. I honestly thought their time clock was out of sync or broken. The 5K went extremely well. I finished without any problems, even though there was no way I would win the race.

I was reading the "Bible in a year" for the twelfth time at this point, and I switched from a written version of the Bible that I was reading to an audio version of it because I was still struggling with double vision. I found that I had forgotten many things as a result of my strokes, but I was surprised by the fact that I lost almost no memories of what I read or studied in the Bible. This even applied to memories from childhood.

*****

I tried to go fishing that summer with one of my nephews, Jacob Logan. I had trouble casting the line because I had lost so much of my body strength because of my four strokes. I also slipped on the steep banks while walking and fell and bruised my tailbone. Dr. Bowlus told me during an examination for my strokes that this would hurt for several months.

*****

My wife and I gathered all the telephone numbers of select neighbors who agreed to help me if something went wrong, and I needed help getting to the hospital while my wife was at work. We then made sure that all the phone numbers had been put on my telephone. Fortunately, the only time that I had to call a neighbor for help was to help catch my dog. She had gotten outside of the fence and was harassing another neighbor's chicken coop. The dog was just too fast for me to catch because of the four strokes. We also had to be assisted by my stepson, Seth.

*****

In early May 2019, Lt. Tim Amstutz, the jail administrator of the Allen County Jail, and Sgt. Todd Gresham, the assistant jail administrator, reluctantly stopped by my house and informed me that the sheriff, at the time, was going to force me to retire by the end of the month of May 2019. The chief deputy sent me a letter on January 25, 2019, explaining that I was authorized twelve weeks of time under the Family Medical Leave Act (FMLA). My twelve weeks had passed. Even though I had several months' worth of sick time left and with Lt. Amstutz and Sgt. Gresham disagreeing with the decision, the sheriff had made the decision to force me to retire. I was informed that I could resign without a pension and hope to be awarded disability and receive a fraction of what my sick time was worth or be fired and receive nothing for my sick time and receive no support from the sheriff's office for seeking a disability pension. I reluctantly agreed to resign. I was initially going to try to go back to work and was going to ask if I could start at half days, but I had to retire.

The next day, my wife and I had an appointment in Columbus, Ohio, at the headquarters of the Ohio Public Employees Retirement System (PERS) to file for a disability pension. We traveled to Columbus that evening and stayed with Carol's niece, Sabrina Kell, and her future husband, Shaun Swayne, because our appointment was early in the morning. We filed for the option of five years of disability and then were reassessed for permanent disability upon the advice of our case worker because we had a better chance of being awarded this option. We would wait about four months to find out the final decision of the PERS Board.

Before we returned home to Lima, we went next door to Ohio Deferred Compensation to withdraw some funds that I had invested there. They withheld the appropriate amount for federal taxes and mailed us a check for the rest of the amount about a month later.

*****

It hurt me for a long time that the sheriff's office would treat me like this, especially after recently having been named Civilian Employee of the Year for 2018 and having written a book about the men who have served in the office of sheriff.

I later tried to extend my health insurance from work through COBRA (Consolidated Omnibus Budget Reconciliation Act). During the last telephone call I had with the insurance company, I became extremely frustrated and upset because I was not getting any help. I told the man who answered the telephone what had happened with the four strokes. He said that he did not have an answer for me, but he would stay on the line and guide me through the system until we got an answer. We eventually got the problem worked out. In the future, I only needed to continue with COBRA health insurance for one month before my family qualified for Medicaid. I also individually qualified for Veterans Administration (VA) medical coverage. I use it for secondary coverage.

That summer, I also cut myself on a piece of glass while doing dishes. I bled badly because of my blood thinner. I researched on the Internet afterward and found out that the administration of cayenne pepper or red pepper on a wound would quickly stop the bleeding. Months later, I cut myself again and found out that this really works. It stopped the bleeding in less than a minute, and it did not sting.

I also found that food without salt was much blander until I got used to it. After I got used to eating food without salt and started using garlic and seasonings from the Big Axe Spice line, the food started tasting better.

That summer, I also made a serious attempt at vegetable gardening. I grew green beans, cucumbers, cherry tomatoes, and regular size tomatoes. After tasting how fresh they were in comparison to grocery store vegetables, Carol was hooked on gardening also. We would grow these and other fruits and vegetables in future years.

*****

I also began attending the men's prayer group at church that summer. It was the group that had visited me in the hospital when I was a patient. We met on Tuesday mornings at 7:00. The group had started years earlier and has met for over nine years as of the publication of this book. The group varied in size and membership over time, but it was about fifteen in number at its largest. I was a member for several years. Even though I was no longer strong with group communication skills, I still got a lot out of the group.

*****

In July 2019, Carol and I started going to the Veterans Food Pantry once per month. This is a local charity. During the next several years, we probably received eighty percent of our meat and a portion of our canned goods from the Veterans Food Pantry. There were other food pantries available, but neither Carol nor I wanted to take food regularly that cost us nothing. We figured that I had served overseas in the US Navy for over six years as a younger man, so I had made some sacrifices, so I was entitled to go to Veterans Food Pantry. It felt good to help provide my family with some of its food again through my efforts.

*****

Bill Harthun, my friend from church, who helped drive me to appointments, saw Dr. Bowlus also. He started scheduling appointments consecutive to mine and then began attending my appointments. This enabled him to report back to my wife more accurately. This continued until I was able to drive again.

*****

I also planned to camp in the side yard of my home with Selah and Melody that summer. My wife decided to join us. Both stepdaughters ended up canceling, so my wife had to sleep on the hard ground without the girls being present. My small group from church enjoyed ribbing my wife about our camping trip in the side yard.

God also began putting it on my heart to write a book talking about how God had carried me through my then four strokes. I was still afraid that I would die at any time. I questioned whether I would be able to finish a book if I started to write one. I decided to try anyway. My eyes were not in a state to tolerate writing a book, but I did write a number of short essays that were several paragraphs in length and recorded key events. These essays were invaluable for accuracy when I later did start writing the book.

*****

I found out that my application for disability had been approved by PERS on August 22, 2019, for a period of five years. I would be evaluated in 2024 to determine if my disability would become permanent. I was extremely relieved to find out about this, but it was approved two days before my fifth stroke.

*****

The City of Lima put in a water line down our street that summer. We tapped into the water line and had greater water pressure almost immediately.

*****

We also went to the Allen County Fair for the veteran's ceremony while the water line was being installed. We also went to the gospel tent to listen to the concert that had been scheduled for that evening. The concert was scheduled for the evening before my fifth stroke.

CHAPTER 5

When Dr. Almudallal, my neurologist, told me that I would have a fifth stroke and die after reviewing my MRI, my wife and I researched the Internet for anything that might help.

The following are some of the vitamins, supplements, and strategies that we found. These substances and strategies should not be used by the reader unless approved by your physician. These items are presented in no particular order of importance.

Shrinking Arterial Plaque—Harvard Medical School, in its Postgraduate Medical Education online course titled "Nutrition Management: Treating Cardiometabolic Disease," states that you can reduce the size of arterial plaque through the use of drugs called statins as well as eating a Mediterranean type diet, such as consuming medium to high amounts of whole fruits and vegetables, whole grains, nut and legumes, olive oil, and poultry and fish, with limited amounts of red meat, alcohol, and dairy.

The accompanying study is discussed more in depth in the International Journal of Cardiology, February 1, 2019.

Fish oil. New research found that fish oil supplements lead to a significant reduction in stroke and heart attack risk (University of Utah, December 17, 2019).

Folic acid. National Library of Medicine searched PubMed, EMBASE, and the Cochrane Library through October 2016 and demonstrated through meta-analysis that folic acid supplementation is effective in stroke prevention in patients with cardiovascular disease.

CoQ10. St. Luke's Hospital in Chesterfield, Missouri, reports that CoQ10 works as an antioxidant and may reduce damage following a stroke.

Vitamin D3. The Journal of Clinical and Diagnostic Research reported on February 1, 2017, that vitamin D supplementation in post-stroke patients is helpful in the prevention of recurrent stroke.

Weight. Healthline Editorial Team reported on June 1, 2019, that maintaining a healthy weight and a healthy body fat ratio or body mass index (BMI) is a good way to manage many risk factors for stroke.

Magnesium. PubMed, EMBASE, the Cochrane Library, and ClinicalTrials.gov were searched through January 15, 2019, and demonstrated that for each 100 mg increase in magnesium taken daily, the risk for total stroke was reduced by 2%. I took a 250 mg tablet daily.

Garlic. India.com reports on October 3, 2019, that garlic contains a molecule called *ajoene*, which prevents blood platelets from accumulating in one place and forming a blood clot, which is known to cause a stroke.

Ginger root. Vondt.net reported in the study "Ginger Can Reduce Brain Stroke Damage by Ischemic Stroke" that ginger had a neuroprotective effect against brain damage caused by oxidative stress that can occur, among other things, in ischemic stroke, where anemia leads to too little oxygen (hypoxia) in affected tissues. This study was completed in 2011 by Wattanathorn, et al.

Turmeric curcumin. Bmccardiovacdisord.biomedcentral.com reported on March 1, 2018, in their study "Curcumin Prevents Stroke in Stroke-Prone Spontaneously Hypersensitive Rats by Improving Vascular Endothelial Function" that treatment with curcumin significantly delayed the onset of stroke and markedly increased the survival time of patients, supporting that diet can change and may be an effective way to prevent stroke and suggesting turmeric as a good choice for patients at high risk of stroke.

L-arginine. WebMD reports in the study "L-Arginine Improves the Symptoms of Strokelike Episodes in MELAS" that L-arginine dilates and relaxes the arteries. This in turn causes the artery to expand.

Probiotics. According to PubMed, the *Iran Journal of Medical Science* (January 2018) reported that probiotic supplements might be useful in the prevention or attenuation of brain ischemic injury in patients at risk of stroke.

The Cleveland Clinic reported in March 2020 that probiotics are made up of good bacteria that help keep your body healthy and working well. These good bacteria help you in many ways, including fighting off bad bacteria when you have too much of them, helping you feel better. Probiotics are part of a larger picture concerning bacteria and your body—your microbiome.

Apple cider vinegar. Umoyo Natural Health reports that apple cider vinegar is a natural laxative, and it can improve digestion, lower blood sugar levels, improve insulin sensitivity, increase satiety and help people lose weight, reduces belly fat, lower cholesterol, and lower blood pressure and improve heart health. I took two capfuls mixed with my breakfast drink every morning.

Cinnamon. According to the US National Institutes of Health on August 10, 2018, eating cinnamon helped lower blood pressure. WebMD reported on October 13, 2020, that cinnamon has been shown to reduce total cholesterol levels.

Dr. Bowlus told me that 100 was a normal score for LDL cholesterol or bad cholesterol. He told me if I could get that number down into the fifties, I could slowly reverse the damage from my strokes. I take three 1,000 mg tablets at breakfast. Cinnamon does not have to be taken in tablet form. It can be used in its natural form.

Citrus fruits. WebMD reported on February 12, 2012, that the flavanones in citrus fruits can lower the risk of suffering a blood-clot-related stroke by 19% in women. The British Journal of Nutrition reported on February 28, 2016, that individuals drinking a glass of orange juice per day saw their risk of a brain clot drop by 24%. The Dutch National reported that consumption of a glass of fruit juice every other day lowered the risk of stroke by 20%. The American Heart Association reported on February 12, 2012, that eating higher amounts of a compound in citrus fruits, especially oranges and grapefruit, may lower ischemic stroke risk.

Green tea/black tea/coffee. NPR reported on March 15, 2013, that researchers found in a study by the American Heart Association that the more green tea a person drank, the more it reduced the risk of stroke. It can lower the risk of stroke by 20% in green tea drinkers who drink four cups daily. Sciencedaily.com reported on March 4, 2009, that drinking at least three cups of green or black tea a day may significantly reduce the risk of stroke. According to new research, the more you drink, the better your odds of staving off a stroke.

The Institute for Scientific Information on Coffee reported a further meta-analysis of nine cohort studies published in 2012 and concluded that coffee consumption of four cups of coffee or more per day showed a preventive effect on stroke. In the European subgroup, increased coffee drinking showed an 18% reduction in the risk of stroke.

I do not like coffee and did not drink enough green tea or black tea to lower the risk.

Cayenne pepper. This is also called red pepper. The *Baltimore Sun* reports on May 27, 2001, that if you have a cut that is bleeding, put ground cayenne pepper on it. The bleeding will stop quickly. I do not feel that it stings.

Bananas. Bethel Medical Associate reports that bananas are packed full of potassium—an important blood pressure-lowering mineral. Potassium helps balance sodium in the body. The more potassium you eat, the more sodium your body gets rid of.

Avocado. Ndtv.com reports that avocados are packed with oleic acid, which can reduce high blood pressure and cholesterol levels.

Flaxseed. WebMD reports that some call flaxseed one of the most powerful plant foods on the planet. There is evidence that it may help reduce your risk of heart disease, cancer, stroke, and diabetes.

Chia seeds. The AndersonCompanies.us report that the fatty acid from flaxseeds, chia seeds, walnuts, shrimp, and brussels sprouts helps improve brain health and lowers your risk of stroke.

Walking. Harvard Health reported on November 1, 2014, that more research confirms that regular walking helps to prevent stroke.

Metformin. Ncbi.nlm.nih.gov reports that epidemiologic studies have shown that metformin reduces stroke incidence and severity. Although diabetes and hyperglycemia are well-known risk factors for stroke, the beneficial effects on stroke outcomes are independent of their glucose-reducing effects. I was prescribed this medicine briefly, and it may have reduced damage from my fifth stroke.

CHAPTER 6

Following breakfast on August 24, 2019, I started walking. As I started to walk, my dog began to bark uncontrollably. I walked to the dog kennel in our garage to see what was happening. I dropped what I was carrying and bent down to pick it up. When I stood back up, it seemed like I was looking through broken glass. I believe that my dog had sensed the onset of my fifth stroke. My vision did not get better over the next several minutes, so I went to lay down. My wife then went to work for several hours at the bread store where she worked at the time. When she got back home, my vision was still blurred, so I had her take me to St. Rita's Medical Center.

*****

Following some medical tests being completed, the doctor assigned to me determined that I had had a fifth stroke. I had a right frontal lobe stroke. I now was one of those rare patients who had strokes in two different systems of the brain. Dr. Bowlus later joked that I was an anatomy lesson from medical school.

I remembered that I had a bad case of hiccups periodically throughout the previous week. I later researched this on the Internet and found out that this can be a sign of a stroke.

Unlike what was predicted by Dr. Almudallal, I had not died when I had my fifth stroke.

Doug Boquist, my pastor, was out of town on sabbatical, so Brad Taylor, my church's executive pastor, immediately came to St. Rita's Medical Center and prayed for me. This was very comforting to me. A hospital chaplain later visited me and also prayed.

The hospital staff transferred me to 4A Neuroscience where I spent a couple of days. I remember being attended by a male nurse who had grown up in a house about two houses away from where I had lived in Delphos, Ohio, prior to me getting married.

While I was on 4A, I had a transesophageal echocardiogram (TEE) to check for abnormalities in the heart valves and chambers. This procedure was conducted by Dr. Nallu.

During supper one evening, I was visited by Dr. Arthur. He asked me if I was interested in coming back to 7E

Rehabilitation for treatment. I answered that I was interested. The next day, I transferred back to 7E Rehabilitation.

My blood thinning medication was changed from Eliquis 5 mg twice daily to Pradaxa 150 mg twice daily. My Atorvastatin 40 mg daily stayed the same. My vision was extremely blurry, and I was a little weaker on my left side.

This was my fifth time through treatment. I needed physical therapy, occupational therapy, and speech therapy. In physical therapy, I worked a lot to improve my gait and strengthen my leg muscles. I also worked on improving my fluidity of motion and sitting down and standing correctly. In occupational therapy, I worked with TheraBands to strengthen my arm muscles. I also continued my work with Jamie Dickman, OT, on improving my double vision. I went to the outpatient therapy building and worked on the Dynavision to prepare for taking the computerized driving test again. Carol and I did not stay in the functional apartment again since we had been there so recently. In speech therapy, I continued working on memorizing lists of items and trying to repeat them back to improve my recall. In one exercise, I listed as many of the fifty states as I could remember. I did not remember all the states, but I did fairly well, considering that I had gone through five strokes. I also worked on problem-solving exercises.

I may have had a second TIA. I felt extremely light-headed and out of sorts. Staff had me lay down. Dr. Arthur put me on an IV for several hours. I then talked with Dr. Chan Seng Tan, my neurologist. I also remember talking to him about starting double therapy on a different occasion. He wanted to add Plavix 75 mg daily to my Pradaxa. He said that he had never put anybody on this combination of medications. He said that it would be risky, but I said that I was willing to try it.

Whenever I used the bathroom at night, I used a urinal and left it for the nurse to empty out. If I had to take a bowel movement at night, I had to call the nurse because the bed had an alarm to sense movement. I again had to transfer from my bed to the walker. After I walked across the room, the nurse or nurse's aide had to help me transfer to the toilet.

I celebrated my anniversary while I was in the hospital. I asked Brittany Patterson, OT, to take me to the hospital gift shop so I could buy Carol a card. I also asked her to pick up a gift card on the way to work, but she would not let me pay her for it later. I thought she was wonderful to do this for me.

When Carol came in with her gift, she also had a snack and some balloons. One of the balloons was shaped like a heart. It held its helium for a number of months after my discharge from the hospital. We liked to say that it was symbolic of our love for each other.

One Sunday, Carol did not arrive for several hours after the time that she thought that she would. She did not call, and I started to worry. When she arrived, she told me that the water had gone out at the house. Our plumber, Jon Burkey, went to church with us, and he had the part that we needed at his house, so he repaired our plumbing on a Sunday afternoon. Someone else at church paid the bill. We were never told who this person was. I was amazed that people would look out for my family in this manner.

I also made a sign one evening in recreation therapy with Kellie Saine. It was stained brown and read in white letters *Give Thanks to the Lord*. It still hangs over the sliding glass door in our house. I also went to the eighth floor and played euchre with Kellie Saine, and some patients from that floor.

*****

My sister's son, Jacob Logan, was also married while I was in the hospital. I had originally intended to attend the wedding, and I would have had I not been in the hospital. Several relatives emailed pictures of the ceremony to me.

*****

I had been in the hospital for sixty-four nonconsecutive nights by this time in 2019. I would spend one more night in the hospital for a post-stroke sleep study. This would account for sixty-five days by the end of 2019.

Following discharge from the hospital, my pharmacy had trouble with their Pradaxa order twice in a row, and I had to move that medication to another pharmacy.

*****

I continued with my walking after I arrived home from the hospital. I shortened the distance I walked, and Carol walked with me for a week or two to make sure that I did not have problems. I did not have problems, so I began walking on my own at my regular distance of 3.1 miles or 5 kilometers.

*****

I found that my garden was overgrown, but there were still a lot of beans and cucumbers to harvest. I had already been harvesting the tomatoes before the stroke.

Several weeks later, I started case management for my disability with Managed Medical Review Organization (MMRO) from Michigan. I had a telephone conference about my disability every several months. This continued throughout my five years of disability. Eventually, my case management changed to Commonwealth Medical from Massachusetts in December 2021 after Ohio PERS ended its contract with MMRO. My case worker would be responsible for my reassessment in 2024.

*****

I again entered St. Rita's Medical Center's outpatient treatment program. It was my sixth time in treatment. This time, I only had physical therapy and occupational therapy. The speech therapist felt that I would not benefit from further speech therapy. Discharge notes from physical therapy dated October 28, 2019, reported "difficulty with ambulation due to weakness and decreased balance." Medical records from September 13, 2019, indicated that I did a number of exercises similar to the last time that I used the outpatient gym for physical therapy. In occupational therapy, medical records from October 17, 2019, indicated that I made "progress toward goals with grip strength and coordination. Reports the reading is going well. Demonstrating bilateral UE (upper extremities) dynamic standing tasks with supervision. Reaching various heights from above shoulder to below knees. Driving evaluation scheduled for 10/23/19." I did better on the driving test when I took it the second time. I still was limited to local driving and was not allowed to drive on the interstate or at night.

*****

When I was in US Navy boot camp, I had two drill instructors who seemed fixated on us not fainting and falling down during close-order drills and causing our company to lose points. They always told us to make sure our knees were not locked, and that we rocked back and forth slightly so our blood would keep pumping. We used to practice how not to fall down. I thought that it was ridiculous at the time, but after the strokes, I had doctors comment on how little I fell down. Many times, I would catch myself checking to see that my knees were not locked and that I was rocking back and forth slightly to make sure that I had good blood flow.

*****

My wife and I both feared my imminent death. This caused me to get rid of some possessions so she would not have to get rid of them if something happened to me. I remember how difficult it was for my father to go through his father's possessions after he died because he had stubs from bills that were over fifty years old. I determined that this was not going to happen to Carol if something happened to me. I started getting rid of books in our attic, including old high school yearbooks and a book from US Navy boot camp about my stay there. I got rid of a couple of boxes of old postcards from my childhood. I also wrote an "open in case of" letter to Carol. The letter contained final thoughts and contained a page with account numbers and life insurance policies.

I also found a company that issued a policy that paid a large portion of the value of our mortgage on the house if I died. Prior to paying two years of premiums, the company refunded what a person had paid in premiums. It was not cheap, but I was obsessed with Carol's care if something happened to me. After all, my disability would stop if I died. Carol would only be eligible for the remainder of my pension fund after my disability payments were deducted.

*****

A local cemetery was also having a sale of plots in the veteran section. Plots only cost $90 if you were a veteran, so I bought one. It was kind of strange viewing what would be your final resting place. If I died first, then I would be cremated. Most of my ashes would be put in an urn and buried. Some of my ashes would be buried with Carol. She already had a cemetery plot next to her first husband. If Carol died first, then all my ashes would be buried in the urn. It is difficult to plan for your own death.

*****

I also went to the VA to be examined for new glasses. The VA optometrist gave me a referral to a civilian ophthalmologist, Dr. Brian Chinavare, at Pajka Eye Clinic in Lima. The VA optometrist saw what she thought looked like cataracts. I did have cataracts forming, but Dr. Chinavare did not think they were bad enough to be removed yet. He also found protein growth on my right cornea. He was able to remove it with laser surgery. While this did not eliminate all my vision problems, the results were an immediate and dramatic improvement in my vision. I was able to see much better out of my right eye. When I walked, I was able to see flags in the far distance that I did not even know were there previously.

*****

I went to see my chiropractor, Dr. Feltz, about once a month. Stroke patients are generally not advised to see a chiropractor. Besides helping cure a problem with pain in my right arm, it helped with my range of motion. It made it much easier to walk. I just made sure that he did not do any high-velocity adjustments on my neck. He adjusted my neck with an activator.

*****

I began to volunteer. I started to serve as a mentor one morning a week in a classroom for males in the county alternative school. The men's group that I attended at church participated in this project.

I also started volunteering at Our Daily Bread Soup Kitchen with Don McClure and Bill Harthun from church.

We did inventory, stocking shelves, and recycling in the back of the facility, usually on Fridays.

I also began volunteering as I had previously with Special Friends Ministry at church. We worked with special needs children so their parents could attend church, knowing that their special needs child was safe. Pam McClure, Don's wife, headed this ministry. She also headed Buddy Break, a new ministry that I joined. Buddy Break provided respite care for special needs children once quarterly.

I also joined a Kairos team. Kairos is a nondenominational movement that brings the Word of God into the state prison system. The event consists of a Thursday through Sunday weekend that functions similarly to an Emmaus Walk. We were scheduled to hold a Kairos event near the end of March 2020. We had several Saturday training, but then the event was canceled by the Ohio Department of Rehabilitation and Corrections because of what was then a little pandemic known as coronavirus or COVID-19. The prison system opened up briefly during the late summer of 2021. We were going to hold a Kairos event, but we had to cancel the event again because of a surge in COVID-19. We would not be able to hold a Kairos event until June 2022.

About that time, I spoke to Dr. Arthur at St. Rita's Medical Center about volunteering on 7E. I filled out a volunteer application, but it was put on hold for about eighteen months because COVID-19 shut the hospital down to volunteers.

My volunteering at the alternative school was suspended as schools started providing Internet education because of COVID-19.

That Thanksgiving, I volunteered to work at the community dinner at the Allen County Civic Center that my church had taken over sponsoring. My wife and two stepdaughters worked also. It was a lot of work, but it was extremely rewarding.

*****

I tried to grow tomatoes in my garage that winter. I was not very successful at it because I did not have the room and all of the proper equipment. I did have one tomato plant that survived the winter and thrived in the outside garden after I transplanted it in the spring.

CHAPTER 7

On March 23, 2020, about one week before the world went into full lockdown because of COVID-19, I had just eaten breakfast and taken my blood pressure like I did every morning. My blood pressure was within the normal range. I was in the restroom getting ready for my day, and my double vision suddenly got worse. I made my way back to the kitchen and took my blood pressure again. It was still in the normal range.

*****

Rather than take a nap, I had Carol take me to St. Rita's Medical Center. Doctors found that I had mild dysarthria (a mild speech disorder characterized by poor articulation), mild facial weakness on the left side, partial gaze palsy (ocular nerve palsy on the left lateral gaze), diplopia (double vision) starting at 8:40 a.m., disequilibrium, and facial droop.

By this time, staff from the emergency department at St. Rita's Medical Center were used to me, and it seemed like they knew just what to do. I remember having a remote consultation with Dr. Alenzi, a neurologist from St. Vincent's Hospital in Toledo, Ohio. Emergency department staff did an MRI on me and sent me to 4A Neurology without waiting for results.

I remember watching the movie *Overcomer* while I was on 4A. My nurse on both days was Nurse Kelsey Hampshire. It seemed like my symptoms were clearing up, but I was told that I needed to wait for Dr. Ali Almudallal, the on-call neurologist to see me the next day. I thought that I was going to be told that I had a TIA, but the next day, Dr. Almudallal told me that I had had a sixth stroke—a small stroke in the right caudate head. Dr. Almudallal added aspirin 81 mg to my medication regimen for one month. He also replaced my Atorvastatin 40 mg daily with Rosuvastatin 40 mg daily. He said that he expected me to fully recover to the baseline of my fifth stroke. I found this rather funny since I had been told that I would have a fifth stroke and die.

I remember that I also had bad hiccups for a week prior to this stroke. I had researched this on the Internet following my fifth stroke and found that this could be a sign of a stroke. I do not remember whether I had hiccups for a week prior to any of my first four strokes, but I kept this in mind in case I had a seventh stroke.

The hospital sent therapists to assess how much damage the stroke had done. The first person to assess me was a physical therapist. She had to ask me to slow down my pace while walking because she was having trouble keeping up with my IV pole. That assessment went extremely well. Next, I was assessed by a speech therapist, Jill Unverferth, SLP, whom I knew from earlier treatment. We talked in part about my desire to volunteer at St. Rita's Medical Center in addition to completing the assessment. This assessment went well also. Dr. Almudallal did not even wait for an assessment by an occupational therapist before he discharged me without inpatient or outpatient treatment. Additionally, he had me see Dr. Eugene Lin to consult with him in my treatment.

If a stroke can be easy, then this one was easy. I had the stroke on Monday, was released from the hospital on Tuesday, and walked 3.1 miles (5 kilometers) on Wednesday.

*****

My wife and I were extremely worried, like the rest of the world, about catching COVID-19. There was a rumor that someone who frequented the soup kitchen had been exposed to COVID-19. Since I had just had a sixth stroke, I stayed home from the soup kitchen for about six weeks.

*****

I had been attending the stroke survivors support group, Stroke Club, at St. Rita's Medical Center. Erin Foxhoven, PTA, one of the group's leaders, called me and informed me that the group's meetings had been suspended indefinitely because of COVID-19. The group did not meet again until late summer 2021. It merged with the Traumatic Brain Injury Support Group at that time and changed its name to that. I was asked by Megan Evers, SLP, another leader of the support group, to write out a presentation of my experiences with my strokes to be presented at the October 2021 meeting. Her presentation skills were much better than mine, so she read the presentation for me to the group. I later expanded this presentation greatly and reviewed and summarized one thousand pages of medical records. All that work eventually became the book you are now reading,

*****

For about a year, our church services were held online because of COVID-19. We really missed our church family. Around Easter, we had a drive through Holy Communion at church. We celebrated this by driving up in front of the church and rolling down our windows. The on-duty pastor said a prayer and administered the elements of Communion. We then made some small talk with the pastor. This was our only social contact with our church community. We had to do this for a time because of COVID-19. Members of the choir, of which Carol was part, sang the song *Forever* by Kari Jobe for Easter. They sang the song remotely. Video clips were sent in by all the participants and were merged by a staff member at church. The video was set up similar to the old *Hollywood Squares* game show, with the picture of one person stacked on top of or beside the picture of another person. It was a beautiful production.

*****

My social work license continuing education renewal work for 2020 was basically done before I had my strokes, so it was fairly easy to complete my two-year renewal for my social work license. My continuing education work for my 2022 renewal period was much more difficult. I had a lot of trouble completing the work because of the strokes. Eventually, I decided that I would let my social work license expire in 2022. About six months later, I was uncomfortable with the decision to let my license expire, so I tried to do the coursework again. This time, I was able to complete the work with some difficulty. My continuing education was finally completed in 2021 and was ready when I renewed in 2022.

*****

Jacob Logan, my nephew, and his wife, Caitlin, had their first son, Colton Lee Logan, in 2020. I still remember when Jacob was a baby. It is hard to believe he is a father now.

*****

About this time, I really became interested in listening to Christian music. I listened to K-Love a lot with my telephone and earbuds while I walked. I also listened to YouTube videos of Christian songs for hours with my tablet and earbuds. I listened to a lot of different artists, but one of my favorite songs was "Overcomer" by Mandisa. I really identified with this song. It gave me a lot of hope for the future.

That summer, I painted some concrete geese in my front yard. After my father repaired the antlers on a concrete deer in my front yard, I painted it also. I did not do badly with my paint jobs, but I probably got more paint on myself than the deer.

I again gardened during the summer of 2020. It was a dry summer, and the results of what I actually grew were mixed. That was my last big garden. Gardens would be smaller in the future.

I also found an old dresser at a thrift store. I put on new knobs, and I hired my youngest stepdaughter, Melody, to stain the dresser. She did a good job, but my father wiped down the top of it because it was beginning to puddle. I found out that my father had always been known for his staining of objects when he was a young man.

*****

We did not have much of a vacation in 2020 because of COVID-19. We went to Hayden Falls near Westerville, Ohio, a suburb of Columbus, Ohio. It was nice, but the water was low because it was a dry year.

*****

We also went swimming at Indian Lake, Ohio. My Facebook friends were surprised that I could still swim after having six strokes.

*****

I was not able to walk any 5Ks in 2020 because they were all canceled because of COVID-19, but I continued volunteering at Our Daily Bread Soup Kitchen. Allen County's alternative school and St. Rita's Medical Center were still closed to volunteers because of the pandemic.

*****

Carol and I were involved in several "praytests," which are protests where the participants prayed. We joined *Bless the Blue* through a local church and demonstrated peacefully in support of law enforcement. We both bought T-shirts in support of this cause. We prayed at both the Lima Police Department and the Allen County Sheriff's Office. We also demonstrated peacefully in support of efforts to stop human trafficking. We prayed at a rally at the Allen County Civic Center. We also bought T-shirts in support of this cause.

*****

We also tithed our COVID-19 stimulus checks to God's work. We tithed our income, giving ten percent to our local church. We decided to give a tithe of our stimulus checks from COVID-19 to social and Christian agencies doing work like the church.

*****

This was the year of the Trump-Biden election, so I signed up with the Allen County Board of Elections as a poll worker. I was nervous that I would not be able to complete my tasks at the election polls because of the damage from my six strokes. I did not say anything about the strokes to my coworkers until about ten hours into the shift. After learning about the strokes, my coworkers were surprised that I was able to keep them in the dark about my strokes all day and keep up with the pace with them during such a busy election. I first brought up the subject in a conversation with my assistant voting location manager. She immediately responded that God was not through with me yet.

Other coworkers asked me questions related to avoiding strokes. One coworker methodically asked me questions about surviving a stroke. She was a nurse, whose father had just suffered a stroke several weeks earlier. She was looking for information regarding her father. I answered all the questions as best I could.

*****

I only unfriended one Facebook friend because of the election. This person held different political views than I did. This was not a problem for me even though that person was extremely bitter and negative about the election. Then the person posted on Facebook after the election that anyone who voted differently than they had was a racist. Their message to everyone was extremely hateful. I did not respond to any of their posts. After I was called a racist, I got tired of the negativity and simply unfriended the person. I have my political views, but if a person holds views that are different than mine, I figure it is their right. I just ask that the other person gives me the same respect that I give to them.

*****

Again, I volunteered at the community dinner at Thanksgiving at the Allen County Civic Center. My church was sponsoring the event again in 2020. Because of COVID-19, my church had people pick up their dinner and take it home that year.

*****

My mother was in a nursing home for most of 2020. She had another stroke while in Florida earlier in the year. She went through treatment in Florida and seemed alright after her return to Ohio, but she began having problems where she would slide to the floor and be afraid to get up. I helped my father as best I could. He called the local rescue squad a lot for help, but it eventually became too much for him. He had to send her to a nursing home. We paid her a lot of visits at the window of her room. My father had gotten her a cell phone, which she used with a nurse's help during visits. We were able to have some actual visits with her on campus grounds at the nursing home, but usually, we had to visit her at the window of her room. This was because of COVID-19. My mother had COVID-19 during the summer but remembered so little that she may not have known that she had it. It was a mild case.

Travis Craft, another nephew through my brother, and his wife Megan had their first child. He was a boy, and they named him Jackson "Jack" Edward Craft. My mother knew of her great-grandson but never knew him personally. She choked to death on December 14, 2020. She choked on some food during dinner in her room. Her choking reflex had given her problems because of the stroke. I knew that she was not doing well and would probably die of something soon. I cried a couple of days before she died as I wrapped her Christmas presents, but I have not cried since. I used to have seasonal affective disorder annually and take medicine. I no longer need medicine either. While I have been reminded that I take a lot of supplements now, I truly believe that my third and/or fourth strokes affected my brain in the area that controls depression because I no longer can really experience depression.

My family met at a local restaurant for several years at Christmas. We met after my mother's death, but we did not meet in 2021. We likely will not celebrate Christmas again as an extended family.

*****

I started 2021 by going to the VA for a checkup. In addition to the checkup, I was given a booster shot for pneumonia. Eight days later, I was diagnosed with COVID-19. I went for testing after no longer being able to smell the lemon essential oil I was using during my shower. I had been given the essential oil for Christmas. Several days later, Carol was diagnosed with COVID-19 also. The symptoms of COVID-19 were similar to an extremely bad case of the flu for both of us.

Our refrigerator broke down, so we had to buy a small dormitory-sized refrigerator to get us through COVID-19. Fortunately, it was cold enough outside that the garage was as cold as a refrigerator. The wife of one of Carol's cousins, Jessica Phillips, had to shop for basic items for us at the grocery.

I remember watching a nature video series when I was not sleeping during my recuperation.

Both Selah and Melody had been staying overnight with friends when we were diagnosed, so they stayed with my father, Ronald Craft, after we were diagnosed and went to school from his house until we had recovered from COVID-19. Seth stayed home and was quarantined, but he was never sick. Carol's brother, John Kell, and his wife Kamil Kell from Texas both had a worse case of COVID-19 than we did. They had COVID-19 about a month before we did. John thought that my case of COVID-19 would have been worse if the VA had not given me a booster shot for pneumonia eight days earlier. Later that year in March and April, I received both shots for the Pfizer COVID-19 vaccination. In November 2021, I received the Moderna booster shot for COVID-19.

*****

We went out for dinner for Valentine's Day several days later. We went out several days before Valentine's Day because a snowstorm was coming. We bought matching flannel shirts and wore them for the dinner for the first time. We put pictures on Facebook. This was the first picture that we had taken together since having COVID-19. The picture was well received on Facebook.

One of the important things for 2021 was that my youngest stepdaughter, Melody, participated in and won the Allen County Spelling Bee. This was her second year participating in the event.

*****

Finally, on March 20, 2021, I reached my one-year anniversary of being stroke-free. It was a Tuesday, and I celebrated in a men's small group. We prayed for my health and that I would remain healthy in the future.

EPILOGUE

The VA diagnosed me with two cases of double vision. One case affected my long-range or driving vision, and the other case affected my short-range or reading vision. The VA recommended that I get two pairs of prism glasses and use the appropriate pair. I was told that it is not possible to make a pair of prism glasses like a pair of bifocal glasses that can correct two types of vision. The improvement to my reading vision prism glasses made it much easier to do inventory at Our Daily Bread Soup Kitchen. It also made it possible to write this book. The prism glasses that affected my driving vision obviously made it easier to drive. While my original pair of prism glasses helped my driving vision also, they were getting old and blurry and needed to be replaced.

*****

I also had an infection beneath a wisdom tooth. The tooth had to be removed, or the situation would have become serious. Unfortunately, no one in Lima would remove it because I was on both Plavix and Pradaxa. I had to have it removed by Case Western Reserve University School of Dental Medicine in Oral and Maxillofacial Surgery in Cleveland, Ohio. The wisdom tooth was removed by Dr. Jaclyn Tomsic. I also had other dental work that could not be done in Lima. It was done by Dr. Chisohlm Chukwu. I had to be driven to Cleveland by my father or wife on five different occasions.

*****

I continued my walking. In 2021, I kept track of how far I walked that year. I walked a total of 187.5 miles. There were no 5K run/walks in 2020 because of COVID-19, but there were more 5K run/walks in 2021. I walked four 5K runs/walks that year. I won two finisher's medals and one second place medal for men in my age group.

I had begun making an entry on Facebook for every 5K run/walk, praising God for giving me another day to walk a 5K run/walk. Within seconds after posting my Facebook entry for that 5K run/walk, race officials announced that I had won second place medal for males in my age group. I frantically figured out how to add text and a picture of me wearing the medal to Facebook. I had to announce the winning of the medal to make my post complete.

*****

My oldest nephew, Cory, also my brother's son, and his wife Anja also had a child. She was a girl. Her name was Ella Renee Craft.

Finally, in August 2021, I was able to begin volunteering at St. Rita's Medical Center in the rehabilitation unit where I was twice hospitalized. I primarily do administrative work for Kellie Saine, RT, and Jean Roehme, Rehab Tech. I also do tasks for Amy Bok, RN, MSN, CRRN; Mallory Wildermuth, LSW; and Megan Evers, SLP.

*****

In 2022, the Ohio Department of Rehabilitation and Corrections allowed us to start holding Kairos events. We held a Kairos event at Allen-Oakwood Correctional Institution in Lima, Ohio, in June 2022.

*****

I also continue to participate in the Traumatic Brain Injury Support Group at St. Rita's Medical Center.

*****

I will be reassessed in June 2024 to determine if my disability will be continued or if I will be returned to work.

*****

My faith in Jesus Christ will always reign supreme over everything in my life.

End

ABOUT THE AUTHOR

This picture was taken on June 19, 2022 (Father's Day).
It had been four years since I had been on a bicycle.

Darrell Craft is a devout Christian of the Nazarene faith. He holds an AA, a BA in psychology, and an MSW in clinical social work from the Ohio State University. He is also independently licensed in social work by the state of Ohio. Additionally, he has an endorsement in clinical supervision from the state of Ohio.

Darrell worked for several social work agencies and is retired as the psychological services coordinator at the Allen County Jail in Lima, Ohio. He had his first of six strokes in December 2018. He is now a volunteer for Our Daily Bread Soup Kitchen in Lima, Ohio, St. Rita's Medical Center in Lima, Ohio, and Kairos Prison Ministry at Allen Oakwood Correctional Facility in Lima, Ohio. Darrell is married to the former Helen Carol Gallaspie and has three stepchildren. Darrell and his family reside in Lima, Ohio.